Spelling, Grammar and Punctuation

John Polley

Longman

York Press

YORK PERSONAL TUTORS

titles in series

GCSE English	GCSE Maths
Novels and Short Stories	Number Book 1
Shakespeare	Number Book 2
Film and Media	Shapes, Space and Measures
Poetry	Algebra
Drama	Handling Data
Spelling, Grammar and Punctuation	

YORK PRESS
322 Old Brompton Road, London SW5 9JH

PEARSON EDUCATION LIMITED
Edinburgh Gate, Harlow
Essex CM20 2JE, United Kingdom
Associated companies, branches and representatives throughout the world

First published 2000

ISBN 0582 40426-6

The author would like to thank the following people for help in the preparation of this book: Robin B. Polley, BA, MPhil for the section on Language variation and Alexis J. Polley, MEng, MSc, MPhil for notes on the Internet.

Designed by Shireen Nathoo Design, London
Illustrated by Spike Gerrell, Sholto Walker

Typeset by Gem Graphics, Trenance, Mawgan Porth, Cornwall
Colour reproduction and film output by Spectrum Colour
Produced by Henry Ling Ltd, Dorchester, Dorset

CONTENTS

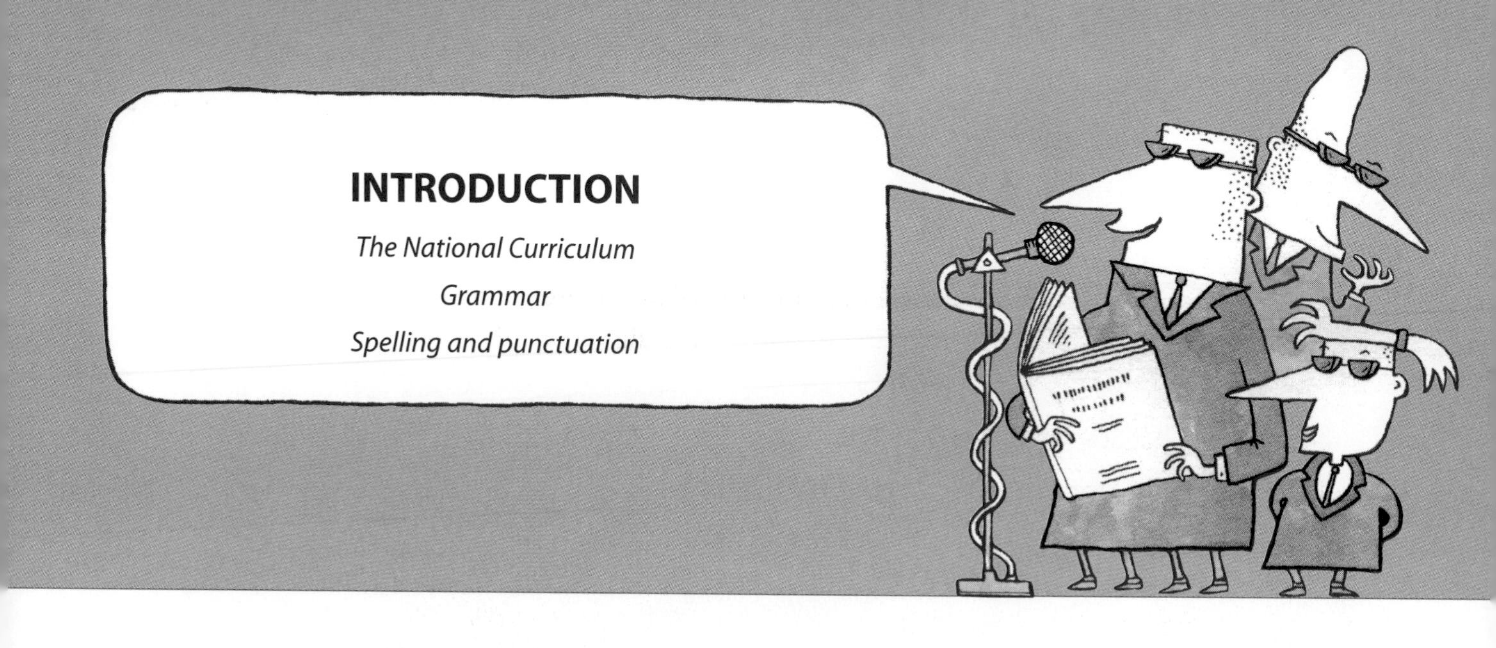

INTRODUCTION

The National Curriculum

Grammar

Spelling and punctuation

This text takes you through the main components of the Standard English and Language Study sections of the National Curriculum.

All languages have their own grammar – the rules and examples which govern the way we use the written word.

There is a variety of approaches to the subject and the one which we shall follow may in places be controversial. Nevertheless, the approach used in this text is the one that most teachers of English currently practising will recognise!

The intention is to make the subject as straightforward as possible given the difficulty of the material. We shall start with a consideration of the different parts of speech arranged in alphabetical order beginning with the adjective. Thereafter we shall look at sentences, clauses and phrases.

It is the writer's experience that there is no single way to achieve excellence in spelling, so a variety of approaches to improvement are examined in the spelling section. The word lists included here are a resource which have proved their value in the classroom.

Accurate punctuation is a very difficult skill.

THINK ABOUT IT

Avoid the greengrocers' temptation – to put an apostrophe wherever a word ends with an 's'.

In this section you will learn the uses of the different punctuation marks with tips that offer straightforward guidance to success.

The National Curriculum stresses the importance of studying the development of English, seeing how it changes over the years and observing the variations between standard English and dialectal variations.

The section on language variation looks at how language is acquired. There is help with understanding terms such as accent, dialect and jargon, with tests that will give you a light-hearted chance to test your ear for language!

In the closing sections of the book, you will be given a brief history of the development of our language and a quick guide to the Internet. The book ends with a collection of tests that give *you* the chance to judge *your* success at grammar, spelling and punctuation!

GRAMMAR

Parts of speech

The sentence

The dirty dozen

Parts of speech

The term, 'part of speech', refers to the various types of word and the job they are doing in a sentence. Confusingly, the same word can be one of a number of parts of speech and you have to look at the word in a sentence to see how it is being used.

Adjectives

An adjective is the name given to a word which qualifies (or describes) a noun. In English, it is generally placed before its noun:

I needed a purple hat.

Adjectives may also stand on their own as complements to verbs.

She looked lovely.

NOTES

Adverbs

As its name suggests, the adverb is mainly used in association with a verb adding to its meaning:

Linford ran powerfully to take first place.

The adverb shows how he was running and is an adverb of manner.

It may also indicate where an action is taking place:

Linford stood there for the medal ceremony.

It may be used to say when something happened:

Linford won yesterday.

These two sentences show the other uses of adverbs: to add to the meaning of other words and to add to the meaning of a whole sentence:

Linford ran breathtakingly fast.
Luckily, he was in top form.

NOTES

The articles

There are two articles in English: the definite and the indefinite. They are also known as determiners.

The definite article is 'the', and the indefinite article is 'a' or 'an'.

You use 'a' before a word that begins with a consonant and 'an' before vowels or a word beginning with an unpronounced 'h':

She ate an egg.
An hour passed before she arrived.

Conjunctions

A conjunction is a word used to join together two clauses. There are two types of conjunction:

- **co-ordinating conjunctions** – which join two clauses of equal value:

  I went home and watched television

- **subordinating conjunctions** – which connect subordinate clauses to main clauses:

  She was allowed out late although she was only sixteen.

You can, of course, write that sentence the other way round but notice how it affects the punctuation.

Although she was only sixteen, she was allowed out late.

NOTES

Interjections

An interjection is another name for an exclamation such as:

Begad! Botheration! Gosh!

Nouns

Nouns are the names of things. There are two main categories:

- **the common noun** – the common noun as in:

  She wore a sweatshirt.

- **the proper noun** – which is always written with a capital letter:

  Tracey wore a Carnegie Hall sweatshirt.

DID YOU KNOW?
The longest recorded place name in the world is Taumatawhakatangihangakouauotamateapokaiwhen-uakitanatahu – it is a hill in North Island, New Zealand.

NOTES

Traditionally, common nouns are divided into three sub-classes:

- **The concrete noun** – i.e. the name of something that can be measured by one or all of the senses:

  He leant the bicycle against a wall.

- **The abstract noun** – i.e. something which exists in the mind:

  He had a great love for his fiancée.

- **The collective noun** – which is self-explanatory:

  An exaltation of larks woke me far too early!

DID YOU KNOW?
Surnames were uncommon in Britain before the thirteenth century and were mainly introduced for legal purposes amongst the wealthy so that they knew who the money was being left to!

NOTES

....

....

....

....

Prepositions

The preposition is a word placed before a noun or pronoun and used to link it to the rest of the sentence:

She stood behind the counter.
The river flowed under the bridge.

A preposition takes the object case ('the counter' and 'the bridge'), something we do not notice with nouns – for in English, **nouns do not change according to whether they are subjects or objects**. We do, however, see the preposition at work when it comes to pronouns, and this confuses many English speakers:

Between you and me, I think something should be said.

Personal pronouns

There are three persons:
'I' is the first person and always written with a capital letter;
'you' is the second person to whom I am talking;
'he', 'she', 'it' and 'one' are the third person.

There are two numbers: singular and plural.

Subject Pronouns

Person	Singular	Plural
First	I	we
Second	you	you
Third	he, she, it, one	they

Object Pronouns

Person	Singular	Plural
First	me	us
Second	you	you
Third	him, her, it, one	them

NOTES

DID YOU KNOW?
The pronoun 'it' in expressions such as 'It's late' and 'It's a pity' is technically a dummy – a word that has little or no meaning but has to exist for the expression to make sense!

Possessive adjectives and possessive nouns

Pronouns may also be used as adjectives and are then known as possessive adjectives as in:

my job	our job
your job	your job
his/her/its job	their job

A pronoun may stand on its own as we can see in this sequence of sentences where the highlighted word is a possessive noun:

That is your chair; mine is beside it.
Yours is wooden.
His and hers are antiques!

Demonstrative pronouns and demonstrative adjectives

Here the words, 'this', 'that', 'these', 'those' stand for a noun which is perceived to be either here or there!

I like this (the ice-cream in my hand) but I don't like that (the plate of spinach I haven't yet finished eating)!

Where we use 'this', 'that', 'these' and 'those' with nouns, they are termed demonstrative adjectives:

These football supporters are friendly with those policemen.

NOTES

Relative pronouns

When we join two clauses, we occasionally use a relative pronoun as a conjunction.

- 'Who' is the subject form and 'whom' the object form: both are used of people:
  She was the girl who started it!
  I was the one whom you saw.

- 'Which' may be either subject or object and is used when referring to non-human things:
  That is the computer which I want.

- 'That' applies to anything you aren't sure about!
  It was the cat that spilt the milk.

- 'whose' means either *'of whom'* or *'of which'*:
  I am the boy whose mother wrote the letter.
  Where is the dog whose muzzle came loose?

DID YOU KNOW?
In the first century BC, grammarians were employed to decipher writing: there were no spaces between words and little punctuation – you had to see patterns in the unbroken lines.

NOTES

Verbs

Verbs are a class of words that refer to action or state. Those which have subjects are termed finite, those without, non-finite.

Those which take objects are called transitive; those which do not are intransitive.

DID YOU KNOW?
Strong verbs are those which change their internal vowel to change tense; e.g. 'I sing' and 'I ring' which become 'I sang' and 'I rang'. But you can say singed as in 'I singed my beard' and ringed 'I ringed the timetable where it applied to me'!

Non-finite parts of the verb

Non-finite parts of the verb are those which do not have a subject:

- **the present infinitive** – e.g. to be
- **the past infinitive** – e.g. to have been
- **the present participle** – e.g. being
- **the past participle** – e.g. been

Past: I did my homework.	Present: I am doing my homework.	Future: I shall do my homework.

N
O
T
E
S

Tenses

English verbs have only two tense endings, for the present and the past:

- **The present tense** – of regular verbs, changes only in the third person singular where an 's' is added:

  I walk, you walk, he walks, she walks ...

- **The past tense** – of regular verbs is formed by adding -ed:

  I walked, you walked, he walked ...

- **The future tense** – is formed in different ways but chiefly by using 'will' or 'shall'. The distinction between using 'shall' and 'will' is less clear nowadays.

  Strictly speaking, 'shall' is used with the first person and 'will' with the second and third persons:

  I shall walk, you will walk, he will walk ...

NOTES

Other tenses are formed using the auxiliary verbs, 'to be' and 'to have':

- **Present continuous** – *I am walking the dog.*
- **Past continuous** – *I was walking the dog.*
- **Perfect tense** – *I have walked the dog.*
- **Pluperfect** – *I had walked the dog.*
- **Conditional** – *I would walk the dog.*
- **Conditional Perfect** – *I would have walked the dog.*

(Notice that this is often incorrectly said and written as if 'have' is 'of'.)

'I must have seen her' might sound like, 'I must **of** seen her'.

BEWARE OF THIS ERROR

KEY CONCEPTS

- Verbs have persons and numbers
- Verbs agree with their subject
- Verbs which take objects are called transitive verbs

NOTES

Moods

There are three moods which affect the general meaning of a sentence, according to whether it is intended to be factual, nonfactual or instructional.

- **The indicative** – is the form of the verb most commonly encountered and presents a statement:

  I hit the cricket ball.

- **The subjunctive** – expresses possibility of some sort:

  God save the Queen.

- **The imperative** – is used for giving orders:

  Leave the room!

Voice

There are two voices – active and passive. Notice how the same idea can be expressed in different voices:

I hit the ball. (active)
He saw the girl. (active)

The ball was hit by me. (passive)
The girl was seen by him. (passive)

The active and passive voices are correctly used but you will notice that the passive sounds rather awkward. There *may* be good reasons why you would want to say 'The ball was hit by me' – maybe because you were being asked what had happened to the ball. In the same way, you can justify the use of the passive in the other sentence. On the whole, it is better avoided: we try to use as few words as possible when we are writing.

NOTES

Transitive and intransitive verbs

- **A transitive verb** – is one that takes an object:

  I saw the child.

- **An intransitive verb** – is one that does not take an object:

  He ran very fast.

Some verbs can be used either transitively or intransitively like the verb, 'to feel':

She felt the material. (transitive) *She felt happy.* (intransitive)

The verbal noun or gerund

A verbal noun is the present participle used as a noun:

I love walking

Strictly speaking, we should use a possessive adjective in the following example:

I was delighted by your giving me a present.

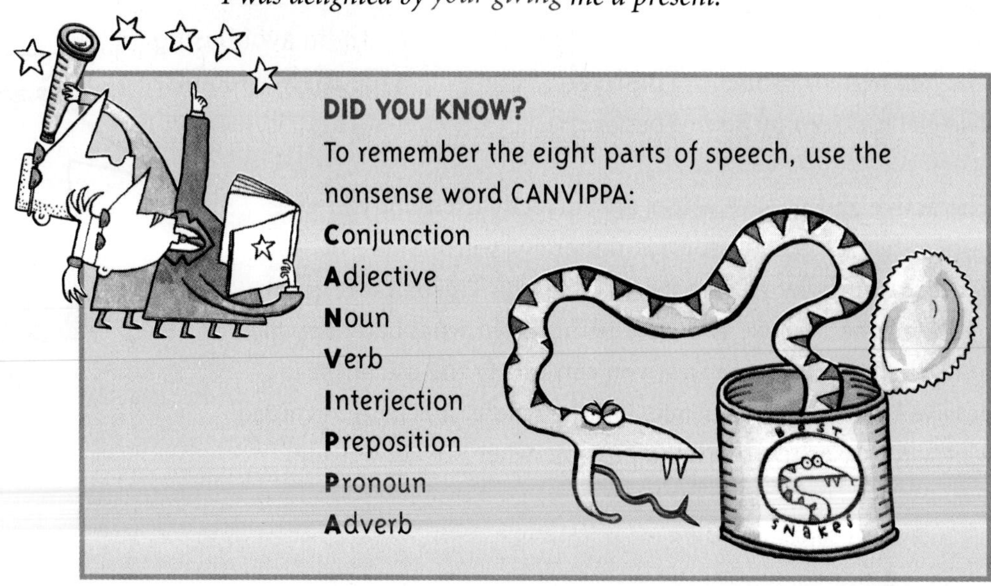

DID YOU KNOW?

To remember the eight parts of speech, use the nonsense word CANVIPPA:

Conjunction
Adjective
Noun
Verb
Interjection
Preposition
Pronoun
Adverb

NOTES

The sentence

It is notoriously difficult to define a 'sentence'. It is easy enough to say that a sentence begins with a capital letter and ends with a full stop. This does not mean that every group of words beginning with a capital letter and ending with a full stop is a sentence!

A sentence is a group of words containing at least one finite verb which conveys a complete thought:

I ran down the road.

It contains a finite verb – 'ran' – and makes sense as it stands.

THINK ABOUT IT

The word 'sentence' comes from the Latin word *sententia* – an opinion

By contrast, *running down the road* has a non-finite verb, *running*, so does not make complete sense since we are left wondering who is doing the running.

There are four types of sentence:

1 The statement: *I ran down the road.*
2 The question: *Is he running down the road?*
3 The command: *Run down the road!*
4 The interjection: *Gosh!*

NOTES

Major sentences

Major sentences are those which can be analysed grammatically. A multiple sentence is one in which there are two or more clauses. **Each clause has to be linked by a conjunction.** This sentence illustrates a co-ordinating conjunction:

I awoke early and went to the bathroom.

It joins what are two main clauses: *'I awoke early'* and *'(I) went to the bathroom'*, and makes each clause equally important. You can go on adding this conjunction and making an ever-longer sentence:

I awoke early and I went to the bathroom and I cleaned my teeth and washed my face and I went downstairs and my Mum had my breakfast on the table ...

You will recognise this type of utterance as being very childlike in tone. That is hardly surprising because 'and' is one of the first building blocks of speech that the young child discovers.

As the child matures, s/he sees that different ideas have different weights, that one is more important than another, that one depends on another and so on. The relationship between ideas is a key feature of written English and it is expressed in more complicated sentence structures.

KEY CONCEPTS

* Sentences must contain a finite verb
* Simple sentences contain one clause
* Conjunctions link subordinate clauses

NOTES

Clauses

A clause is a group of words that contains a single finite verb. Those which begin with subordinating conjunctions are subordinate clauses.

- **adjectival or relative clauses** – these are clauses which describe a noun. They are most frequently introduced by a relative pronoun as a conjunction and are quite easy to identify:

  She is the actress who played the title role.
  I am the person whom you must follow.
  She is the mother whose children did so well.
  That is the book which I bought in Manchester.
  Spot is the dog that saved their lives.

- **noun clauses** – noun clauses do the work of a noun.

As a subject:	*What you said was unacceptable.*
As an object:	*She said that she was going home*
Before a preposition:	*I shall always stand by what I believe in*

DID YOU KNOW?
The use of noun clauses indicates the highest level of writing.

NOTES

- **Adverbial clauses** – adverbial clauses add to the meaning of a verb. In the examples that follow, the clause is in bold and the verb to which it refers is highlighted.

Concession:	*She gave generously to flagsellers* ***although she was poor.***
Condition:	***If you are careful,*** *you will avoid simple errors.*
Manner:	*He laid out the pieces as* ***I had shown him.***
Place:	*He stood* ***where he could be seen.***
Purpose:	*He ran* ***so that he would win the race.***
Reason:	*He needed the food* ***because he was so hungry.***
Result:	*He worked so hard* ***that he went to university.***
Time:	*She went home* ***before I arrived.***

Notice that if you reverse the order of clauses in these sentences, you need to put in a comma to separate the clause from the rest of the sentence:

Although she was poor, she gave generously to flagsellers.

Subordinate clauses begin with a subordinating conjunction.

NOTES

Minor sentences and phrases

- **Minor sentences** – those which do not have a subject and verb but which are nevertheless understandable. These examples make perfect sense in the situation where you hear them.

  Hey up, then!
  Not a hope.
  Not good enough.

- **Phrases** – are groups of words that do not contain a finite verb. Like clauses, they have a variety of functions.

Adjectival phrases:	*The girl with the faulty computer tore her hair out!*
Noun phrases:	*Running a shop is not an easy life.*
Adverbial phrases:	*She stood by the bus stop.* *At the first stroke, the New Year was rung in.*

NOTES

THE DIRTY DOZEN – TWELVE COMMON ERRORS

There are a number of common errors which are exemplified in the list that follows. The grammatical explanation and the corrections are given after each.

1. ✗ *Everyone enjoyed themselves.*
   'Everyone' is singular; 'themselves' is plural.
   ✓ *They all enjoyed themselves.*

2. ✗ *Running down the road, I saw a bus.*
   It is hard to know who/what is running down the road.
   ✓ *As I was running down the road, I saw a bus.*

3. ✗ *People with less than six items should use this till.*
   'Less' refers to volume, 'fewer' refers to quantity.
   ✓ *People with fewer than six items should use this till.*

4. ✗ *He is more cleverer than me.*
   'Cleverer' means 'more clever', so you do not need two 'mores'!
   ✓ *He is cleverer than me.*

5. ✗ *None of these men are intelligent.*
   'None' is singular, 'are' is plural.
   ✓ *None of these men is intelligent.*

NOTES

6. ✗ *No-one sings like she does.*
   'like' is either a preposition or a verb; do not use it as a conjunction.
   ✓ *No-one sings as she does* or *No-one sings like her.*

7. ✗ *There were 50 people there.*
   Figures up to a hundred should not be written as numerals.
   ✓ *There were fifty people there.*

8. ✗ *She laid in bed.*
   You need the past tense of the verb to lie. 'Laid' in bed suggests she produced an egg!
   ✓ *She lay in bed.*

9. ✗ *The reason why she did it was because she was miserable.*
   If you use the word reason, there is no need to use why or because.
   ✓ *The reason she did it was that she was miserable.*

10. ✗ *Sir, can I go to the toilet?*
    Can is used to mean 'am I able ...?' Teachers are not medically qualified to judge such matters.
    ✓ *Sir, may I go to the toilet?*

11. ✗ *The best boxer won the fight.*
    There are only two boxers in a ring. Best refers to more than two.
    ✓ *The better boxer won the fight.*

12. ✗ *I should be grateful if you will write.*
    The sequence of tenses is wrong.
    ✓ Either: *I should be grateful if you would write.* or *I shall be grateful if you will write.*

NOTES

HIGHER PERFORMANCE

Identify the types of clauses highlighted in each of the following:

1. *If you are careful,* you will be successful.
2. *That she did it* was unquestioned.
3. I wondered *why he did it.*
4. It was the cat *that spilt the milk.*
5. *Despite all the trouble I experienced,* I have remained cheerful.
6. He was there *because he was such a keen fan.*
7. I will follow you *wherever you go.*
8. Describe the face of the person *you saw recently.*
9. No-one sang as beautifully *as you did that night.*
10. Speak clearly *so that all may understand.*

Answers

1. Adverbial clause of condition
2. Noun clause subject of the verb 'was'
3. Noun clause object of the verb 'wondered'
4. Adjectival or relative clause
5. Adverbial clause of concession
6. Adverbial clause of reason
7. Adverbial clause of place
8. Adjectival clause omitting the word 'that'
9. Adverbial clause of manner
10. Adverbial clause of reason

Quiz

1. Identify the part of speech highlighted in each of these sentences:

a. There was no saying what he wanted.
b. No-one is sitting in that chair.
c. The supporters behaved like idiots.
d. I hate noise.
e. The bus moved slowly off.

2. Which of the following are major sentences?

a. The teacher said what I wanted to hear.
b. Just in time too!
c. Whatever next!
d. An interesting place you have visited.
e. Happy memories shared.
f. What was his profession?
g. Into the waves he plunged.
h. As I was running down the road.
i. Forlorn – the very word is like a bell.
j. Read the second paragraph carefully.

Answers

1. a. personal pronoun.
   b. demonstrative adjective.
   c. preposition.
   d. verb.
   e. adverb.
2. a, b, f, g, i, j. Note that b is an interjection!

SPELLING

Better spelling

Irregular words

Derivations of words

Better spelling

The rules of English spelling are complicated, for ours is a complicated language, developed down the centuries from a wide variety of influences. Rules exist for us to check whether we have got things right. **Also, remember that there are exceptions to every rule – and these must be learnt too!**

DID YOU KNOW?
The word 'spell' comes from an Old English word meaning 'magic incantation'!

This writer has spent over half a century on this earth and is regarded as an excellent speller, yet only recently have I finally managed to be certain of the correct spelling of 'weird'. I did it by inventing a little sentence which I now never forget: 'We are weird'.

Weird sounds like the first syllable of *we are*. Now I can remember that e comes before i.

NOTES

....

....

....

....

THINK ABOUT IT

If you always pronounce conscience as 'con science', you will never forget the sc in the middle of the word.

The trouble with English spelling is that much of it dates from before the Great Vowel Shift see p 77 of the fifteenth century, so that today's spelling often reflects the way words were pronounced in Chaucer's time.

This is significant since most students tend to spell words as they are pronounced. This can get you in deep water because one in five words is not spelt that way. Unfortunately, many of the words we use most commonly are irregular. This leads to the misleading impression that English spelling is a completely random ordering of letters – which it manifestly is not!

DID YOU KNOW?
Shakespeare had one of the largest vocabularies of any English writer – about 30,000 words.

NOTES

We can do something to improve our ability to put the right letters in the right order but the approach we must use is a mixed one.

We don't learn to spell by looking at words and learning their patterns yet English words are recognisably English. We could quickly pick out the English port in this list: Gdansk, Gijon and Gosport. Moreover, we would probably think that Gdansk was somewhere in eastern Europe and Gijon in western Europe.

DID YOU KNOW?

The best known dictionary of English was produced by Doctor Johnson (1755). He tried to identify best usage of words and did so on the basis of over 100,000 quotations taken from the previous 200 years. He enabled readers to follow the development in meanings of individual words.

N
O
T
E
S

Most of us can remember the miseries of learning spelling lists for homework, yet we may be puzzled as to why this standard teaching practice has had so little effect on our ability to spell accurately.

We need to understand the principles that underlie spelling so that we can apply them to our writing. At the same time, we must not think that, if we cannot spell, we cannot write. Poor spelling rarely prevents anyone from understanding what has been written: it may be an irritation but it is not a terminal condition for a writer! However, the adult world tends to judge harshly a poor speller.

Whenever we write down a word and it is misspelt, there is always a reason. **What we should be asking ourselves is *why* we spelt that word wrongly in that way.** For if we can understand, we can begin to tackle our real problems.

Spelling is a matter of pride. If you take pride in your work, you will want it to be spelt as accurately as possible. You do not want errors to detract from what you are communicating. There is a variety of techniques which you need to employ.

DID YOU KNOW?
The Oxford English Dictionary records that there have been thirty-one different spellings for merry.

NOTES

STRATEGIES FOR BETTER SPELLING

1. Use a simple approach with new words: **Look** at the word **Cover** the word **Write** the word **Check** the word	2. Try to learn as many rules about spelling as possible	3. Learn tricks of memory – 'We are weird' is one of mine you can have for nothing!
4. Get a parent or friend to check your work	5. Read, read and, yes, read so that you constantly see words	6. Examine unfamiliar words carefully – take the word, 'phthisis', for example. It's really odd – all those consonants at the beginning come from the original Greek word meaning 'to waste away'. Yet once you notice this combination of letters, you will begin to see it elsewhere, in phthiriasis, diphtheria and ophthalmia, for instance and this makes you that much more careful – and successful
7. Do word-games: crosswords are very helpful since you can never arrive at a completed answer if the spelling is incorrect	8. Play dictionary games: get a friend to open a page at random and ask you to spell the first ten entries	
9. Whenever you ask for help in spelling a word, always write down the way you think it should be spelt and then compare your version with the one you are given	10. Write down words you know you find difficult and underline the part of it where you always go wrong	11. Have a dictionary at your side

NOTES

Vowels

There are five vowels (a, e, i, o, u) and each of them has at least two possible pronunciations. Remember the infants' chant:

'Its name is Ay but we say Ah. Its name is Ee but we say Eh.'

What they are identifying is different vowel sounds – long or short:

Long: nAme, mEte, rIte, mOw, dUne
Short: fat, pet, lit, hot, dunce

DID YOU KNOW?
Two words in the English language contain all the vowels in order – facetious and abstemious.

Silent E and I

One of the best-known spelling concepts is 'Silent E', to which we can fairly add 'Silent I', since that vowel works in a similar way. The rule here is that the letter E is magical in that it 'charms' a letter into saying its own name.

If we take the word, 'man', we can hear that it has a short vowel sound and when we add the Silent E to make the word, 'mane', the letter 'a' now sounds its own name. In more sophisticated terms, it has changed to become a long vowel sound.

Consider for yourself the following words and how their pronunciation changes if you add an E:

car	*hat*	*bit*
plum	*pat*	*kit*
tun	*rat*	*mat*

NOTES

Now consider what happens when we have a verb ending with a consonant and we add -ing or -ed to make a different part of the verb.

What you will discover is that the Silent E or Silent I is affecting the pronunciation as in:

mating *hoping* *caning* (silent I)
mated *hoped* *caned* (silent E)

In each of these words the first vowel is lengthened by the effect of the E or I that follows.

If, however, we double the consonants, we find that the first vowel remains short:

matting *hopping* *canning*
matted *hopped* *canned*

By changing the vowel sound we have changed the meaning of the word.

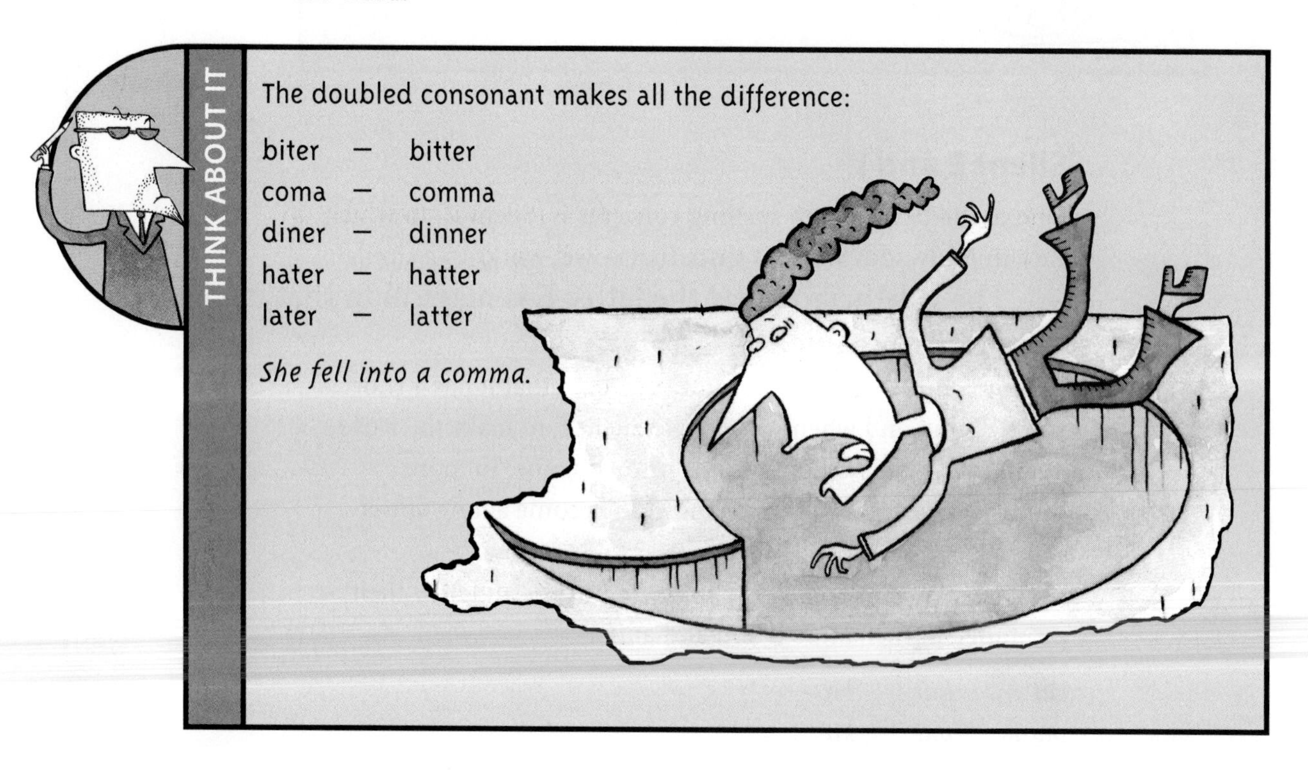

NOTES

E and I also affect consonant sounds by softening them. The two most important effects are seen with C and G, for we know that they can be pronounced either as hard or soft consonants. When either C or G is followed by an E or an I, they soften, as in:

race *rice* *mice*
racing *pacing* *icing*
rage *stage* *page*
raging *staging* *paging*

Then you notice that the I changes the sound of the consonant all on its own. So that when you are adding -ing you can drop the E from the ends of the words – as you don't need two vowels doing the same job. Look at:

race *racing*
pace *pacing*
ice *icing*
rage *raging*
page *paging*
stage *staging*

If, however, you want to stop the I or the E from softening a consonant, you employ an extra letter:

racking *packing* *picnicking* *panicking*

Here the K makes the C a hard sound.

The vowel U has an important use as well since it can stop an E or an I from softening a consonant, particularly a G:

guess *guest* *rogue* *catalogue* *epilogue* *guide*
guile *guise* *guillotine*

NOTES

Consonants

Once you start looking at letters and the way they affect each other, you will begin to make other connections: that J and G are at times interchangeable:

Jeffrey and *Geoffrey, Jillian* and *Gillian*

And that they occasionally alternate:

jelly and *gelatine,* or *jail* and *gaol*

A little further detective work reveals that J as a letter is of quite recent origin. It did occur in Latin as part of the numerals vij (7) and viij (8) and the capital J was not distinguished from I until the beginning of the nineteenth century. In general, the letter J is not used at the end of words – we will see -ge or -dge, as in *rage* or *dodge* – and its use at the beginnings of words is most often before A, O and U where a G would be hard. Other words starting with a J tend to be exotic or American – jasmine, jujitsu, jungle, jive and jeep!

Jasmine jived in the jungle.

NOTES

K is another letter that can alternate, this time with C as in cat and kitten, or Catherine and Katherine. The history of our language is revealed at times by its use. Old English normally used a C for K as in cwic (quick) or cyning (king). It was also pronounced in Old and Middle English before an N though it has now fallen silent but remains as a reminder in such words as knave, knee, knife, know, knuckle amongst others.

DID YOU KNOW?
'K' also distinguishes pairs of homophones (words that sound the same but are spelt differently) such as know/no, knight/night, knave/nave.

Like the J, K has a certain exotic quality, as with words like kangaroo and koala.

Furthermore, K also has a sort of American connection when used at the beginning of trade names – Kleenex, Kwik-fit, or dubious organisations – Ku Klux Klan, to mention but three.

The point about all this is to invite you to start looking at the letters in words to investigate their uses – and it will certainly lead to improved spelling as you do so.

DID YOU KNOW?
Arne Zettersten calculated the frequency of use of individual letters. Here they are, the most frequent first:
E T A I O N S R H L D C U M F P G W Y B V K X J Q Z

NOTES

KEY SPELLING RULES

1 Write i before e except after c, when the sound is 'ee':

believe, thief, chief, grief, ceiling, conceive, receive, receipt

Exceptions: seize, sheikh, weird, weir

2 Words ending in l and adding -ly, then become -lly:

faithful	*faithfully*
beautiful	*beautifully*
loyal	*loyally*

3 Words ending with a consonant followed by y drop the y and add –ies

quarry	*quarries*
ferry	*ferries*
lavatory	*lavatories*

4 Words ending with a vowel followed by y, add an s:

valley	*valleys*
day	*days*
trolley	*trolleys*

5 Words double the final consonant when a suffix is added to a monosyllable:

rot	*rotting*
lob	*lobbing*
instil	*instilling*

6 Words do not double the final consonant if the stress does not occur on the final syllable:

differ	*differing*
interpret	*interpreting*
benefit	*benefiting*

7 Verbs end -ise, nouns in -ice in the following:

practice	*a doctor's practice*
practise	*Athletes practise before races*
advice	*free advice*
advise	*I advise you to go carefully*
device	*a new-fangled device*
devise	*He will devise a test for you*
licence	*a driving licence*
licensed	*He was licensed to drive a taxi*
prophecy	*a witch's prophecy*
prophesy	*I prophesy you will do well*

NOTES

Homophones and Homonyms

- **Homophones** – are words of different meanings that happen to sound the same. Here is a selection:

air/heir	draft/draught
bow/bough	weather/whether/wether
break/brake	lessen/lesson
sun/son	source/sauce
vane/vein	pair/pear/pare

DID YOU KNOW?
Robert Bridges wrote an essay for the newly formed Society for Pure English (1919) in which he identified over 800 entries, with around 1,800 words, that fell under the heading of homophones. He found them to be a burdensome nuisance, often caused by poor pronunciation!

- **Homonyms** – This is a group of words which have different meanings but happen to be spelt exactly the same:

bow, row, lead, pitch

DID YOU KNOW?
The first authoritative pronouncing dictionary was produced by John Walker in 1791.

NOTES

WORDS THAT ARE EASILY CONFUSED

You need to be aware of these words which frequently catch out even the most careful of writers.

A

accept except
access excess
addition edition
advice advise
affect effect
alley ally
allusion illusion
aloud allowed
altar alter
angle angel
ascent assent

B

bale bail
bare bear
bass base
boarder border
boy buoy
bread bred
break brake
breath breathe
buy by

C

canvas canvass
cease seize
cemetery symmetry
cereal serial
cite sight site
clothes cloths
complement compliment
course coarse
cue queue
currant current
cymbal symbol

D

deceased diseased
decent descent dissent
depraved deprived
deprecate depreciate
desert dessert
device devise
die dye
dying dyeing
died dyed
disapprove disprove
disinterested uninterested
draft draught
dual duel

E

eclipse ellipse
elicit illicit
eligible illegible
emigrant immigrant
emigrate immigrate
envelop envelope

F

faint feint
fare fair
farther father
fiancé fiancée
final finale
for four fore
formally formerly
forth fourth
freeze frieze

G

gamble gambol
gilt guilt
gorilla guerrilla

NOTES

Work out ways of remembering differences for yourself

H

hair hare
hear here
him hymn
hoard horde
hole whole
human humane

I

idle idol idyll
imminent eminent
immoral unmoral amoral
immunity impunity
implicit explicit
incite insight
ingenious ingenuous
its it's

L

later latter
licence license
lightening lightning
loath loathe
loose lose
luxuriant luxurious

M

magnate magnet
marshal martial
medal meddle
miner minor
moral morale

N

new knew
notable notorious

P

packed pact
pair pare pear
passed past
peace piece
peal peel
pedal peddle
personal personnel
practice practise
precede proceed
precious precocious
principal principle
profit prophet

Q

quiet quite

R

rain reign rein
recent resent
right write wright
role roll

S

sew sow
stationary stationery
statue stature
steal steel
straight strait
suit suite

T

taut taught
tear tier
their there they're
to too two

W

waist waste
wait weight
ware wear were where
weather wether whether
witch which
who's whose
woman women

Y

your you're

NOTES

Irregular words

Our complicated spelling stems from a variety of causes. The Anglo-Saxon alphabet had twenty-four letters to convey forty basic sounds. After 1066, French scribes re-spelled much of the language, for example introducing qu- for cw- and gh- for h-. At that time, many of the early English printers were foreign and they used their own ideas on spelling. Moreover, after the Elizabethan age all manner of loan words joined our vocabulary, giving yet more variety in spelling.

THINK ABOUT IT

All letters may be used as special symbols, but K and X are used most frequently:

K for kilo, and to catch the eye in Kool Kat.

X is used to denote something or someone unknown as in Mr X; as a shorter form of ex – in Xtra strong; in Xmas where X replaces the Greek letter khi, to signify censorship as in X-rated, and to represent kisses – to mention just a few of its uses.

N O T E S

IRREGULAR WORDS

Here is a list of irregular words that are most frequently misspelt:

A
absence
access
accessible
accommodation
achieve
achievement
across
address
advantageous
aerial
agreeable
although
among
amount
analyse
answer
anxious
appoint
arctic
argue
arguing
argument
assistant
association
athlete
athletics
attach
attachment
aunt
author
autumn
auxiliary
awkward

B
beautiful
begin
beginning
belief
believe
benefit
benefited
bicycle
biscuit
Britain
build
buoy
business

C
calendar
category
ceiling
chimney
chimneys
changeable
commit
commitment
committee
committed
committing
comparison
comparative
conceit
condemn
conscience
conscientious
conscious
coolly
cough
corroborate
courageous
course

D
debt
deceit
deceive
deceptive
definite
definitely
disappear
disappoint
describe
description
desirable
desire
despair
desperate
develop
development
disastrous
discriminate
dissatisfied
dissatisfaction
drunkenness

E
Edinburgh
eerie
eligible
embarrass
embarrassed
embarrassment
encyclop(a)edia
environment
environmental
exaggerate
exceed
excellent
except
excessive
exhilaration
existence
existent

NOTES

IRREGULAR WORDS cont

F
February
forgetful
forgotten
forty
fourteen
friend
fulfil
fulfilled
fulfilling
fulfilment

G
gauge
geography
grammar
grammatical
grief
grievous
guarantee
guard

H
handkerchief
handkerchiefs
harassed
heifer
height
holiday
horrible
humorous
humour

I
immediate
immediately
incidentally
inconvenient
independent
indispensable
innocence
insistent
install
instalment
irrelevant
irresistible
irritable
island

J
jewellery
judg(e)ment
junior

K
keenness
knowledge
knowledgeable

L
leisure
library
lieutenant
likeable
lonely
loneliness
lov(e)able
loveliness

M
maintain
maintenance
manager
managerial
marriage
Mediterranean
Middlesbrough
miscellaneous
mischief
mischievous
misspelling
misspelt
mistake
moustache
murmur
murmuring

N
necessary
necessarily
neighbour
nephew
niece
ninety
noticeable
nuisance

O
occasional
occur
occurring
occurred
occurrence
opportunity
opposite
orchestra
organiser

P
panic
panicked
parallel
parliament
pastime

NOTES

people
perseverance
persist
picnic
picnicking
picnicked
poem
poetry
possess
possession
predecessor
predictable
preliminary
prescribe
prescription
pretty
privilege
procedure
proceed
proceeding
profession
professor
pronounce
pronunciation
pursue
pursuer

Q
quarrelled
quay
queue
queued
queu(e)ing

R
receipt
receive
recommend
repetition
restaurant
rhyme
rhythm
ridiculous

S
secretary
secretarial
seize
separate
sergeant
sheriff
shoulder
siege
similar
sincere
sincerely
solemn
succeed
success
successful
sugar
surprise

T
theatre
theatrical
thorough
till (until)
tranquil
tranquillity
transfer
transferred
transferring
true
truly
tyranny
tyrant

U
umbrella
unanimous
unique

V
vegetable
vehicle
vicious
view
vigorous
visitor

W
Wednesday
weird
whole
wholly
wilful
wilfully
woman

X
xylophone

Y
yacht
yield

NOTES

Derivations of words

Many of our words come from Greek and Latin. By knowing their origins it is often easier to understand how they come to be spelt as they are in modern English. The list below gives the more common elements you will encounter:

	Word	Meaning	Example(s)
A	aer(o)-	air/aircraft	*aeroplane, aerobics*
	agr(o)-	field, farming	*agriculture*
	algia-	pain	*neuralgia*
	ambi-	both	*ambidextrous*
	ante-	before	*antenatal*
	anthrop(o)-	man	*anthropomorphism*
	anti-	against	*antidote*
	aqua-	water	*aquatics*
	arch(ae/o)-	old	*archaeology*
	astro-	star	*astrology*
	audio-	hear	*audiotape*
	auto-	self	*automatic*
B	bi-	two	*bicycle*
	biblio-	book	*bibliography*
	bio-	life	*biology*
C	cardi(o)-	heart	*cardiogram*
	carn-	flesh	*carnivore*
	centi-	one hundred	*century*
	chrono-	time	*chronology*
	-cide	killing	*infanticide*
	-crat	ruler	*autocrat*
	crypto-	hidden	*cryptic*
D	dexter/dextr-	right	*dextral*
	dia-	across	*diameter*

NOTES

The more interest you take in words, the better your spelling

	Word	Meaning	Example(s)
	dict-	say	*dictation*
	-dox	opinion	*orthodox*
	-duct	lead	*aqueduct*
	dys-	bad	*dyslexia*
E	equi-	equal	*equilateral*
F	frater/fratr-	brother	*fratricide*
	-gam(y)	marriage	*monogamy*
G	geo-	earth	*geography*
	-gram/graph	write	*diagram, telegraph*
	gyn(o)/gynae-	woman	*misogyny, gynaecologist*
H	haemo-	blood	*haemophilia*
	hect(o)-	one hundred	*hectare*
	hetero-	opposite	*heterosexual*
	homo-	same	*homosexual*
	hydr(o)-	water	*hydraulic*
	hyper-	beyond	*hyperactive*
	hypo-	under	*hypodermic*
I	iso-	equal	*isobar*
K	kilo-	one thousand	*kilometre*
L	lexis-	speech	*lexicon*
	-lith	stone	*monolith*
	-logy	study of	*geology*
M	mater/matr-	mother	*maternal*
	mega-	many	*megalith*
	micro-	small	*micrometer*
	milli-	one thousandth	*millimetre*
	mono-	single	*monotheism*
	mort-	death	*mortal*

NOTES

	Word	Meaning	Example(s)
N	naut-	sail	*nautical*
	neo-	new	*Neolithic*
	neuro-	nerves	*neurology*
O	oct(o)-	eight	*octagon*
	omni-	all	*omnibus*
	ortho-	core	*orthodox*
P	paedo-	child	*paediatrics*
	pater, patr-	father	*paternal*
	phil-	love	*bibliophile*
	-phobe	fear	*arachnophobe*
	photo-	light	*photograph*
	poly-	many	*polyglot*
	pseudo-	false	*pseudonym*
Q	quad-	four	*quadrangle*
	quasi-	apparent	*quasi-intellectual*
R	retro-	backwards	*retrospect*
	rupt-	break	*rupture*
S	-sci(o)	know	*conscious*
	-scope	viewing	*telescope*
	semi-	half	*semicircle*
	stereo-	solid	*stereoscopic*
T	tele-	from afar	*television*
	the(o)-	god	*theology*
	thermo-	heat	*thermoelectric*
	tri-	three	*triangle*
V	vis-	see	*vision*
	vor-	eat	*carnivore*

NOTES

THINK ABOUT IT

A knowledge of a word's derivation helps to spell it!

American spelling

The USA is one of the very few countries to have successfully introduced reforms to spelling. Credit for this must go to Noah Webster (1758–1843) whose *American Dictionary of the English Language* (1828) laid the foundations of American spelling. His aim was to show the way in which America's independence was reflected in language changes. Not all his reforms were successful but they were far-reaching.

Understandably, there is resistance in Britain to adopting Americanisms, but with American English the standard language of the Internet, we can anticipate encountering more not fewer examples. American spelling is by and large shorter than the British English equivalent, and while British English is tolerated in the USA, the reverse is generally not true.

- **The colo(u)r group** –
  arbor, armor, endeavor, favor, flavor, odor, tumor,

- **The centre/center group** –
  fibre/fiber litre/liter meagre/meager
  sombre/somber theatre/theater

- **OE and AE words** – The oe and ae letter combinations are invariably reduced to a single e:
  oe: estrogen, ameba, diarrhea, fetus, fetid
  ae: archeology, gynecology, encyclopedia, hemorrhage, medieval

NOTES

- **Final L group** – Where verbs end with a single l, they will not be doubled when tense endings or other suffixes are added:

  travel *traveled, traveling, traveler*
  compel *compeled, compeling*

- **-ise versus -ize endings** – Some verbs can only end in -ize, such as seize, capsize. In others, only the -ise ending is possible: advise, surprise.

  Where verbs may end either way, British English is flexible and allows either spelling, whilst American English always stipulates the -ize ending.

  British publishers have their house styles and settle for one spelling or the other to avoid confusion. York Press, the publishers of this title, for instance, advocates the -ise spelling where alternatives exist.

- **Words ending in -ogue** – American words usually automatically drop the closing letters in such words: dialog, monolog, catalog, analog, pedagog and prolog are some examples.

DID YOU KNOW?
In 1992, the world's top three languages were:
Mandarin Chinese – 726 million speakers
English – 427 million speakers
Spanish – 266 million speakers

NOTES

IMPROVE YOUR SPELLING

1. Try to understand why you spell inaccurately. When you make mistakes, it is because you have wrongly applied something you know about the relationship between the sounds of letters and their arrangement in a particular word.

2. Use any trick you can devise to fix spellings in your mind.

   The word 'separate' has A RAT in it.

   Necessary is like an old-fashioned shirt, it has one C and two Ss, a Collar and two Studs.

3. If you cannot hear the second vowel in medicine, and are unsure what it is, think of medic.

4. Have a dictionary at your elbow and use it but before you check on a word try to spell it for yourself.

5. Exaggerate the pronunciation of words to remember their spelling, breaking the word into syllables like

   COM-MIT-TEE

   RHO-DO-DEN-DRON

6. Improve your handwriting.
   The more beautiful your writing is the more likely you are to be keen on getting the spelling correct.

You will not become a brilliant speller overnight but once you start being bothered about it, you are taking a huge step towards eliminating the commonest errors. If you can tackle those, then your spelling will look pretty sound.

NOTES

HIGHER PERFORMANCE

1

Look up the meanings of these pairs of words in a dictionary and explain the differences.

luxuriant	luxurious
official	officious
sensible	sensitive
fictional	fictitious
precipitate	precipitous
uninterested	disinterested
obsolete	obsolescent
silhouette	shadow
repellent	repulsive
biennial	perennial

2

Mrs Malaprop was a character in *The Rivals* by Sheridan who tried to impress by using long words, sadly wrongly! Identify the malapropisms in the following:

1. The doctor did not conclude the insistent patient was a kleptomaniac.
2. He bought his wife a ring of diamonds and haemorrhoids.
3. Geometry teaches us to bisect angels.
4. His toothache drove him to extraction.
5. Our grocery bill is gastronomic.
6. Having only one wife is called monotony.
7. The French troops were slowed down by their amour.
8. I would rather work out of doors than in a sedimentary occupation.
9. An equal-sided triangle is termed equatorial.
10. She was a prawn in his hands.

Answers

1. hypochondriac 2. emeralds. 3. angles.
4. distraction. 5. astronomical. 6. monogamy.
7. armour. 8. sedentary. 9. equilateral. 10. pawn.

Quiz

Select the right word in these sentences:

1. They were not allowed/aloud to go out.

2. She stood their/there/they're looking puzzled.

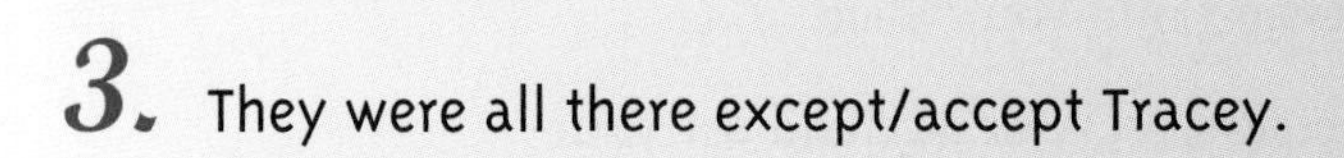

3. They were all there except/accept Tracey.

4. They where/were afraid of what they might find.

5. He was born and bred/bread in Yorkshire.

6. It was so cold you could see your breathe/breath.

7. I would like to complement/compliment you on your success.

8. My personal/personnel opinion is that it is wrong.

9. Friends do not dessert/desert their friends in trouble.

10. I am not sure whether/weather you will like this.

Answers

1. allowed.
2. there.
3. except.
4. were.
5. bred.
6. breath.
7. compliment.
8. personal.
9. desert.
10. whether.

Punctuation is the most difficult of all writing skills to master.

Written English (better known as standard English) and spoken English are entirely different languages.

When you speak to someone, your aim is to convey precisely the thought in your head. You have a number of ways other than using words which help you to realise this aim:

- You are able to put expression into your voice
- You can change the expression on your face and use your hands for emphasis
- And if all that does not succeed, you have immediate feedback – if your listener does not understand you, s/he can just look blankly at you and say, 'What are you on about?'

When you write, however, you only have written words at your service. Into them has to go all the expression you need to make sense.

Look at the sentence that follows and see if you can make sense of it:

I saw a man eating tiger.

If the sentences – for there are two – had been correctly punctuated, it would have made perfect sense:

NOTES

I saw a man eating tiger.
(Not a very digestible meal, I would have thought.)

and

I saw a man-eating tiger.
(All right from a distance!)

THINK ABOUT IT

Punctuation is not used to show pauses in speech or where you take breaths.

This is the commonest source of error and comes from teaching in the early years when you are only concerned with putting down your thoughts. As you develop your mastery of standard English, you become aware that written and spoken English are different languages.

NOTES

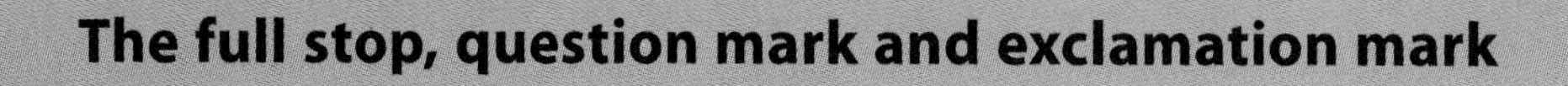

The full stop, question mark and exclamation mark

Each of these has a full stop incorporated in its design:

. ? and !

By using these punctuation marks with some thought you can subtly affect the meaning of a sentence. Look at the three examples given below and see how the change of punctuation mark has created sentences with different meanings:

She wore a hat.
(A plain statement of fact)

She wore a hat?
(It seems unlike her to cover her head in this way)

She wore a hat!
(Fancy her wearing a hat, of all things!)

Using these punctuation marks thoughtfully allows simple expression to convey shades of meaning. The moment you start to do this with words you are beginning to anticipate the response of a reader to your words and that is the first step to sophistication of expression.

KEY CONCEPTS

- There are ten punctuation marks in English
- Punctuation conveys sense
- Punctuation is mainly used to separate units of grammar

NOTES

The comma

The comma is used to achieve clarity in expression. In general, uncertainty with the comma is easy to detect: students who use the pepper-pot method tend to sprinkle them liberally around their writing in the hope that one will occasionally fall in the right place.

A good way to approach the comma is never to use one on your first draft.

Now, when you have completed your piece of writing, read back through it and see where any confusion might arise. A simple example of this approach can be seen below:

I like fish and chips and strawberries and cream.

Now it hardly takes a genius to see that this sentence envisages the writer seated before a remarkably odd meal, yet the first two items and the second two items would for most people represent fairly attractive food favourites. The answer is therefore simple: separate the first two from the second two and hey presto! the confusion is sorted.

I like fish and chips, and strawberries and cream.

NOTES

Incidentally, this disobeys quite neatly one of the rules that people proclaim so loudly about using commas – never have a comma before an 'and'. You need them on some occasions and not on others. It depends on the sense.

DID YOU KNOW?
Sometimes you can have a comma before an 'and'. It is then called an Oxford comma, and publishers often use it.

Other conventional uses of the comma are:

– to separate phrases from the main sentence, in much the way that brackets are used i.e. in pairs:
  Mr Prendergast, our new teacher, was a man from a strange background.

– to separate subordinate clauses from main clauses:
  Before you leave for home, check you have remembered what you need for homework!

– to separate the name of the person addressed from the rest of the sentence
  Here, Harry, what do you think you are doing?

Don't sprinkle commas around liberally in the hope that a few of them will fall into the right place!

NOTES

The colon and the semi-colon

Two punctuation marks which demand care in their use are the colon and the semi-colon.

- **The colon** – has a definite strength to it with its satisfying doubling up of full stops. Its main use is to introduce a list of phrases see p 23

  He was surprised at what he saw: a pile of old clothes; a discarded briefcase; a trail of wet footsteps; and scuffmarks at the edge of the river.

- **The semi-colon** – separates lists of phrases in much the same way that a comma separates lists of words.

  A further use of the semi-colon is to separate short sentences that are closely linked in meaning.

  She arose quickly; threw on the first clothes she could find; quickly brushed her teeth and almost jumped out of the window in her haste to leave the scene.

Inverted commas (speech and quotation marks)

The prime use of inverted commas is to indicate written English words that have been used in a speech. If you are quoting within a quote, the inverted commas are employed systematically to signify both the quotations as in the following sentence:

"I read 'Hamlet' last night," she proclaimed proudly.

In this example 'Hamlet' is the quote within the "I read ... last night" quotation.

The rule is that everything that is spoken is enclosed in inverted commas,

and the following sentences illustrate their correct use in a variety of sentence constructions:

NOTES

'Where are you going?' he asked.
He asked, 'Where are you going?'
'Where,' he asked, 'are you going?'
'Where are you going?' he asked. 'My mother wants to speak to you.'

A further point about indicating speech in your writing concerns its layout. You must always start a new paragraph with each new speaker, however short the speech:

'Where are you going?'
'Who, me?'
'Who else?'
'Home!'
'Just as I thought.'

Laying out speech in this way has a second benefit: it saves you continually having to write, 'he said ... she said ... he said ... she said'.

An important tip is to use speech sparingly. It is far better to quote only what is important and significant to your writing.

NOTES

The dash

Limit your use of this punctuation mark since it is tempting to put it in everywhere you need a comma or a colon. It has the effect of introducing something which is quite surprising, so its overuse can be a little wearing.

Finally I could stand the weird noises at the door no longer and opened it to find – my cat!

The apostrophe

The apostrophe has two uses: to indicate omission of a letter or letters and possession.

- **apostrophe for omission** – e.g. 'he's' instead of 'he is'. In general, the apostrophe for omission is rarely seen in standard English since the contracted form of words is a speech idiosyncrasy.
- **apostrophe for possession** – e.g. 'I had Shelley's book'. The apostrophe for possession is quite simple in theory and quite hard in practice. An apostrophe and an 's' are used on the name of the possessor as below:
  I had writer's cramp.

  In the following sentence, the possessors are in the plural (the pupils) so the apostrophe is added. When it sounds unnatural to have 's' followed by an apostrophe and another 's', the second 's' is discarded.
  The pupils' books were seen by the inspector.

NOTES

HIGHER PERFORMANCE

1 Try punctuating this letter to change its meaning:

Dear John,

I want a man who knows what love is all about. You are generous, kind, thoughtful. People who are not like you admit to being useless and inferior. You have ruined me for other men. I yearn for you. I have no feelings whatsoever when we are apart. I can be forever happy – will you let me be yours?

Debbie

2 Now try punctuating this sentence:

Where he had had had I had had had had had had had had been correct.

Answers

1. Dear John,
   I want a man who knows what love is. All about you are generous, kind, thoughtful people who are not like you. Admit to being useless and inferior. You have ruined me. For other men, I yearn. For you I have no feelings whatsoever. When we are apart, I can be forever happy. Will you let me be!
   Yours,
   Debbie
2. Where he had had 'had', I had had 'had had'. 'Had had' had been correct. (Geddit?).

Quiz

Punctuate these sentences so that they make sense:

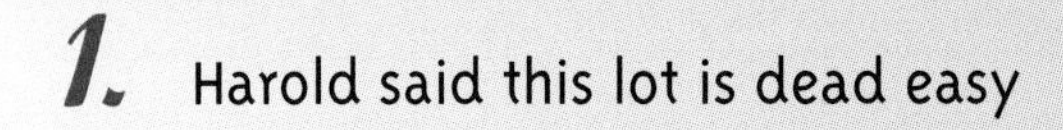

1. Harold said this lot is dead easy

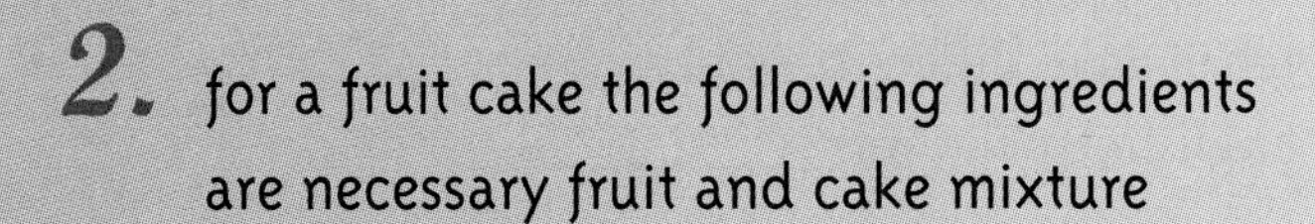

2. for a fruit cake the following ingredients are necessary fruit and cake mixture

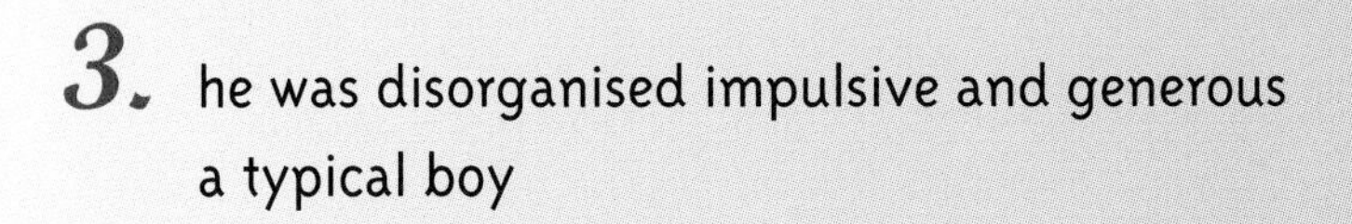

3. he was disorganised impulsive and generous a typical boy

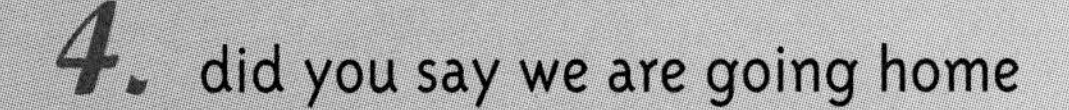

4. did you say we are going home

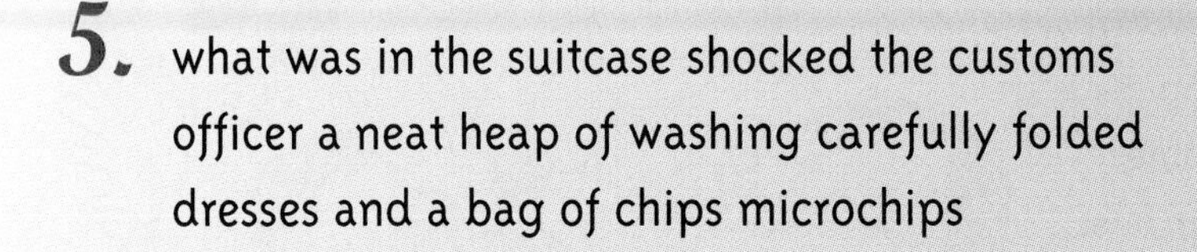

5. what was in the suitcase shocked the customs officer a neat heap of washing carefully folded dresses and a bag of chips microchips

6. she loves hamlet

Answers

1. Harold said, 'This lot is dead easy'. (inverted commas)
2. For a fruit cake the following ingredients are necessary: fruit and cake mixture. (the colon)
4. He was disorganised, impulsive and generous - a typical boy! (the comma, dash and exclamation mark)
5. 'Did you say, "We are going home"?' (inverted commas, question mark)
6. What was in the suitcase shocked the customs officer: a neat heap of washing; carefully folded dresses, and a bag of chips - microchips! (colon, semi-colon, dash and exclamation mark)
7. She loves Hamlet.(the character) or She loves 'Hamlet'. (the play) (inverted commas)

LANGUAGE VARIATION

Early learning

Accent and dialect

Slang and idiom

There is not just one but many Englishes. The differences have to do with who we are, where we live and what we are trying to say or write. In this respect English is no different from any other language. Variations in English depend on:

- individual knowledge and capability
- geographical location
- social situation
- peer group

There is another crucial factor that determines the ground rules: whether the language is written or spoken.

In ordinary conversation we are usually face to face with other speakers: we can interrupt, repeat, ask for explanation, point, use facial expressions, shout and use many more ways to get our ideas across. What happens is so instant and unpredictable that speech is noted for false starts, mistakes, unfinished sentences, changes of direction, hesitations and so on.

NOTES

If we wrote as we spoke, it would be difficult and irritating to read. The reader would not have the chance to stop you and ask what you mean, so you have to be more careful and make language choices that you think s/he will understand.

Early learning

As babies we see our parents responding with rewarding smiles and noises to everything we do. Then comes an awareness that making loud noises ourselves brings things that we want: food, a hug, clean nappies.

Soon we realise that our parents want us to copy their noises, that these noises stand for the things you see around you, then that they can refer to things that you can't see. The process of learning language has begun!

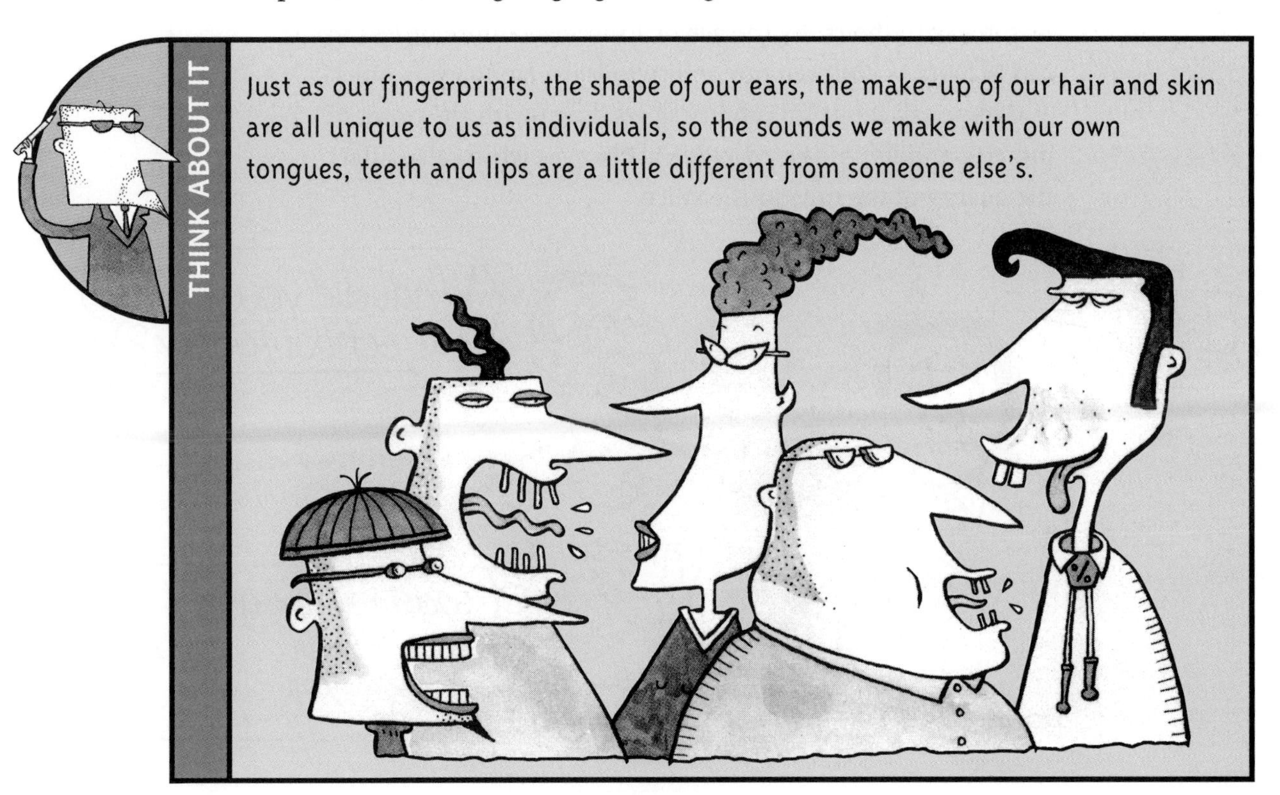

NOTES

As we grow up and meet new people, make new friends, experience new situations, we learn new words, mostly by imitating the sounds that the people around us make and 'sounding' our words in a way we think that people will understand. We even develop the ability to change the sound we use in different situations or with different people. In this way we develop the unique individual sound that is our voice. This sound reflects all the experiences, words and people we have met or heard. It is our accent.

Accent

Everyone has an accent. Throughout our childhood we are unconsciously developing our sound to fit in with the people we live and need to get along with. So our sound shares some features with theirs. By the age of 15 we have more or less fixed our accent. As children our ability to learn language is quick and responsive; but this ability slows down with the onset of puberty and its associated physical changes which also affect the quality of the tone of the voice.

N O T E S

As you have seen, your accent reflects the sounds of the people around you. People who live elsewhere have instantly recognisable ways of speaking.

Throughout your life you classify the sounds you have heard and use, and from your stock of sounds and tunes, choose which you will use in a given situation. The tone quality of your voice will be unmistakably your own – even the most skilful actor finds it very difficult to conceal this. **The accent you use will probably be identifiable as typical of the region you live in, or where you learnt most of your English.** It will probably vary depending on whether you are speaking formally or informally, or whether you are talking with parents, or friends, or foreigners.

If everyone has one, then all languages have as many accents as there are speakers! Since it is impossible to investigate all speakers of a language, it is practical to look at representative groups.

NOTES

Regional labels are only a convenient – and sometimes misleading – way of grouping accent types. It is usual for one regional type – very often the area of the capital, the centre of power and government – to become the 'national standard'. It is a short step from a national standard to its being an indicator of prestige and status. **For this reason speakers using the standard English accent come from all over the British Isles.** The standard accent has lost its regional identity and origins, and there is a danger that all non-standard accents may be seen – mistakenly – as sub-standard accents.

DID YOU KNOW?

In Britain the centre of power has historically been associated with the court of the sovereign, which in the past moved from Winchester to Oxford to London. So the standard English accent has developed as a mixture of south eastern English varieties. The south of the country has always been associated with the court and power and status, and along with this attitude has come the idea of a north-south divide.

NOTES

Dialect

Whereas accent is the term used for the distinctive individual or regional sound of the voice, dialect is used to refer to all of the language features that identify someone's regional or social background.

A dialect has its own grammar, syntax, vocabulary, accent.

The question then is, if dialect includes grammar, syntax, vocabulary and accent, what is the difference between it and language? The answer has to do with the difficulties of 'labelling' that we referred to earlier. A starting point is understanding or intelligibility. It seems reasonable that if two people understand each other we can assume that they are talking the same language. If the understanding is only with difficulty then it is probable that they are using different dialects of the same language.

But Norway, Denmark and Sweden are separate countries and they must have separate languages because we speak of Norwegian, Danish and Swedish. Yet they understand each other. Norwegian, Danish and Swedish are in fact dialects of Scandinavian.

NOTES

Slang

We said that language variations stem from individual, regional or social factors. **Social contexts affect the vocabulary choices we make.** If we want to be accepted in a new situation we may change our language choices so that we seem and sound to be right for the situation.

Speaking casually with friends we use the words that they all use. And usually, these will be words that are not used in the formal standard language. You might well talk about someone as an 'old geezer' or 'feller' or 'bloke' or 'guy' where you would use 'man' or 'person' if you were speaking more formally. This is called 'slang'.

DID YOU KNOW?

Cockney rhyming slang is almost a language in itself:
"I got on the dog and bone to my old china because he was in a two and eight."

Translation:
"I got on the phone to my friend (china plate = mate) because he was in a state."

NOTES

Idiom

Another variation in vocabulary is idiom. This type of language most clearly differentiates the native speaker from the foreigner. The French speak of 'watering the corridor' to mean 'having a drink'. What is particular about idiomatic usage is that it is a more or less fixed string of words whose meaning is contained within the complete phrase

it is a more or less fixed string of words whose meaning is contained within the complete phrase

So 'Put a sock in it!' means something quite different from 'I put my foot in it'; and to say 'I put my socks in it' would just not be understood – unless you were talking about doing your washing.

KEY CONCEPTS

- Dialect identifies one's regional or social background ✱
- Slang consists of non-standard vocabulary ✱
- Idiom is a unit of meaning ✱

NOTES

HIGHER PERFORMANCE

Identify in which part of the country you might hear the following dialect expression:

1. Ah thought Ah knewed ee when Ah seed ee, but Ah knewed Ah knewed ee when Ah yeard ee spik.
2. On Saturday I went sharpen with me mum, bor.
3. Weh ganning te the Toon for a canny neet oot.
4. Yan ... tean ... tethera ... fethera ... pimp.
5. How bis going, snow?
6. Eyt t'pudding afore t'main coourse.
7. In the summer, the grockles are like emmets.
8. Wersia sensa yuma?
9. Catch yerself on.
10. 'Ere have a butcher's at his barnet.

Answers

1. Devon: I thought I knew you when I saw you, but I knew I knew you when I heard you speak.
2. Norfolk: On Saturday, I went shopping with my mother, mate.
3. Geordie: We are going to Newcastle Football club for a nice night out.
4. Cumbria, Yorkshire, Northumberland: the numbers one to five.
5. Bristol: How are you, mate?
6. Yorkshire: Eat the (Yorkshire) pudding before the main course.
7. Cornwall: In summer the tourists are like ants.
8. Liverpool (Scouse): Where's your sense of humour?
9. Northern Ireland: Think about it!
10. Cockney: Look at his hair.

Quiz

'Translate' these expressions, the first five come from the Potteries, the remainder from Derbyshire.

1. Bay chum spiders.

2. Bill Joe nice.

3. Chaise 'n' Pittles.

4. Kine slice.

5. Ar ter toke crate.

6. Looks black ovva Bill's motthaz.

7. Ar dunner know wot ay saze inner/innim.

8. Bitterorate.

9. Loderode rammil.

10. Aze back afooer aze bin onny weer.

Answers

1. Beechams powders.
2. Build your own house.
3. Cheese and pickles.
4. Council House.
5. How to talk right – the language of the Potteries.
6. It will rain soon.
7. I don't know what he (she) sees in her (him).
8. S/he looks attractive.
9. That is rubbish.
10. He is back quickly.

THE DEVELOPMENT OF ENGLISH

Historical influences

The Renaissance

Modern times

English has been spoken in Britain for over fourteen centuries though **there have been so many changes in sounds, vocabulary and grammar that its earliest form is effectively a foreign language**

Look at the following lines. They are from the Old English version of the story of Caedmon from Bede's *Ecclesiastical History of the English People*:

> þa he þæt þa sumre tide dyde, þæt he forlet þæt hus þæs gebeorscipes ond ut wæs gongende to neata scipene, þara heord him wæs þære neahte beboden, þa he ða þær in gelimplice tide his leomu on reste gesette ond onslepte þa stod him sum mon æt þurh swefn ond hine halette ond grette ond hine be his noman nemnde: 'Cedmon sing me hwæþwugu'.

which roughly translates as:

When that he did on a particular occasion, he left the feast-house and was going out to the cattle shed, the care of which was entrusted to him that night, when at the appointed time he laid down his limbs in rest and fell asleep. Then, a certain man stood below him in a dream, and hailed and greeted him by name and called 'Caedmon, sing me something'.

NOTES

Early foreign influence

The first invaders of Britain arrived during the sixth and seventh centuries. They came from different dialect areas in Germany: the East Saxons, South Saxons and West Saxons who live on in Essex, Sussex and Wessex. Predictably enough the East Angles were located in East Anglia, whilst the Middle Angles settled in Mercia and Northumbria.

The institution of Christianity in England following the arrival of St Augustine from Rome in 597 AD was a important feature of our early language development. The monks were the first writers using the Roman alphabet and they provide us with textual evidence of the earliest Anglo-Saxon dialects, primarily from Wessex, Mercia and Northumbria.

The Scandinavian raids from the eighth century and the subsequent settlement of the Danelaw – a line running from Chester to London – effected a sort of north/south divide. Some of the linguistic legacy of the Scandinavians can be seen in place names: the endings such as -by (farm or town), -thorp (village), -thwaite (clearing) and -toft (homestead)

NOTES

DID YOU KNOW?
There are over 1600 Scandinavian placenames in England, especially in Yorkshire and Lincolnshire e.g. Whitby, Grimsby, Lowestoft, Scunthorpe

The Scandinavians also influenced our vocabulary bringing with them 'both', 'same', 'get' and 'give' and the -s ending of the third person verb forms. Family names too can be distinguished – those ending in -son can be identified as being from counties settled by Scandinavians.

The next major influence on the language came with the Norman Conquest in 1066. **This spelt the end of Old English and the major new influence was French.** This was the language of the law court, if not of the criminal. Of potentially greater nuisance value for the modern student were the changes in spelling. The Norman scribes listened to the English they heard and rendered the sounds on paper using their system of spelling. This is when we discover a number of curious spellings entering the language – the -gh in night and enough, an 'o' instead of a 'u' in 'come', 'love' and 'son'.

The Normans brought with them a vocabulary that was derived through Old French from Latin. Very often it duplicated words that already existed in English from Anglo-Saxon. Some words disappeared in this process, others remained to offer different meanings, as with 'pork' and 'pig' or 'beef' and 'cow'.

NOTES

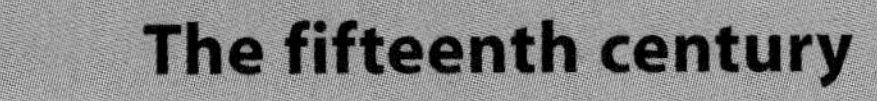

The fifteenth century

Throughout the fifteenth century, in the process known as the Great Vowel Shift, the pronunciation of the language changed significantly towards sounds that our modern accent recognisably developed from. Some sounds from this time survive in various regional dialects.

DID YOU KNOW?
David Crystal in *The English Language* (Penguin, 1988) gives an example of how the sound of the language was altered. The sentence, *'so it is time to see the shoes on the same feet now'* would have sounded like this in Middle English: *'saw it is team to say the shows on the sarm fate noo'.*

It is little wonder that we experience spelling problems when we realise that we are faced with spelling that reflects pronunciation from 600 years ago!

The next key date is 1476, when William Caxton introduced the printing press.

It led naturally enough to standardisation in spelling but more importantly it offered greater opportunities for people to write.

DID YOU KNOW?
In the first 150 years of printing, nearly 20,000 books in English appeared.

NOTES

The Renaissance

The other major influence in the development of the language was the Renaissance, which lasted from the invention of the printing press to the middle of the seventeenth century. This was basically a renewed interest in classical languages – Latin and Greek – and as new ideas were discussed, there was a need for new language where there was no English equivalent.

Britain was not just a nation of scholars, but also of explorers, traders, administrators, scientists, doctors and writers. Some idea of the variety of imported or loan words can be seen when we consider just a few of the words which surfaced in our language at this time, with their origins included in brackets:

criterion (Greek)
macaroni (Italian)
bazaar (Persian)
impersonal (Latin)
cockroach (Spanish)
harem (Arabic)
bayonet (French)
port (Portuguese)
yacht (Dutch)

The two key influences in the closing stages of the Renaissance were William Shakespeare (1564–1616) and the King James Bible, or Authorized Version (1611). Shakespeare put so many words and expressions into print for the first time that he has had a lasting effect upon our daily lives. The Authorized Version of the Bible gave us a whole wealth of idioms such as 'an eye for an eye' and 'the blind leading the blind'.

NOTES

The eighteenth century

By the time we reach the eighteenth century, we are beginning to see modern English. It was Doctor Johnson who epitomised what was happening with the language. He undertook the task of drawing up a dictionary of over 40,000 words defining and illustrating the use of words during the previous two centuries. This mammoth task took him seven years to complete and the publication of his dictionary (1755) stabilised language in a way that had not hitherto been achieved.

Following Johnson's dictionary, there were two prominent grammarians – Robert Lowth and Lindley Murray – who were to have a lasting effect. Their grammars became standard textbooks in schools.

DID YOU KNOW?

While Dr Johnson was writing his dictionary, the War of the Austrian Succession ended (1748); excavations at Pompeii began (1749); Halifax, Nova Scotia was founded (1749); Franklin invented the lightning conductor, and 1752 saw the publication of *The Treatise on the Theory and Practice of Midwifery* by Dr. Smellie.

NOTES

The nineteenth and twentieth centuries

In the last two centuries English has become a world language. The British Empire retreated in the middle of the twentieth century but it left English wherever it had been. It is reckoned that a third of the world's population, over two billion people, use English regularly in their daily lives, and with the fastest-growing form of communication, the Internet, having English as its basic language, English is certain to be ever more popular in the future.

English is a living language, continually changing to meet the needs of a changing world. Creative writers, poets and playwrights have always challenged the rules or conventions of English expression and this has led to changes in language.

DID YOU KNOW?

English is the language of the air. An Italian airline pilot landing in Rome talks to the Italian air traffic controller in English.

N
O
T
E
S

We have to remember that people feel passionately about our language and seek to protect it from any change, as that is felt to be a corruption of our precious linguistic inheritance.

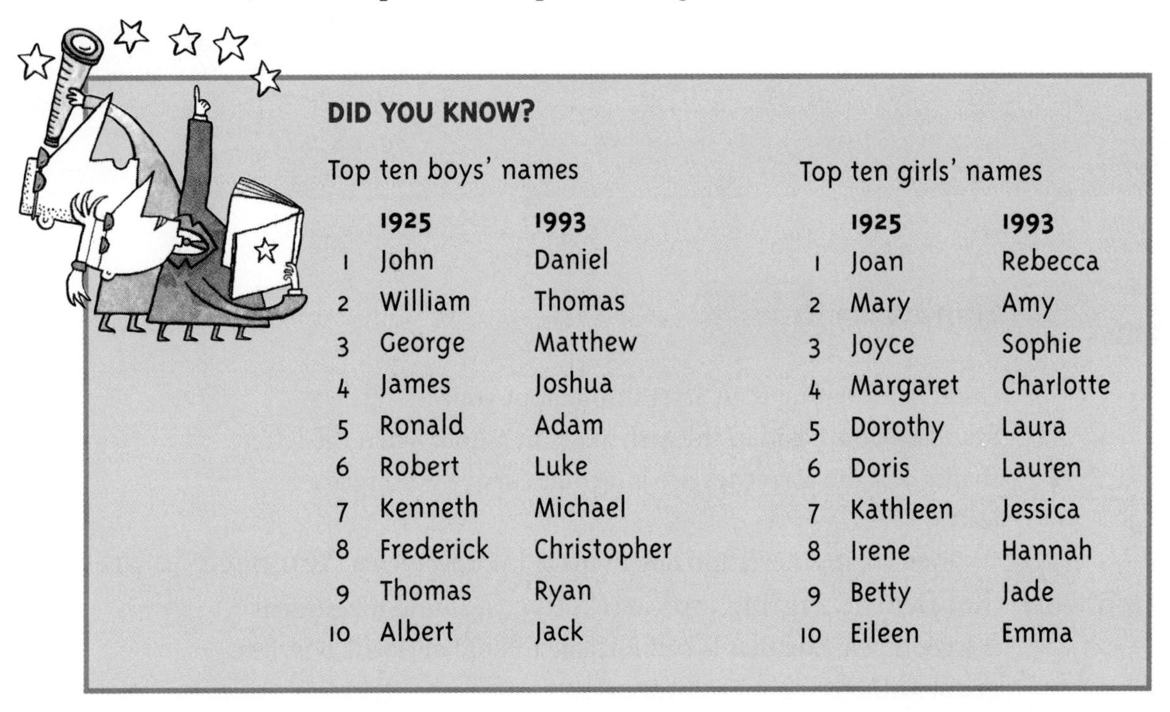

DID YOU KNOW?

Top ten boys' names

	1925	1993
1	John	Daniel
2	William	Thomas
3	George	Matthew
4	James	Joshua
5	Ronald	Adam
6	Robert	Luke
7	Kenneth	Michael
8	Frederick	Christopher
9	Thomas	Ryan
10	Albert	Jack

Top ten girls' names

	1925	1993
1	Joan	Rebecca
2	Mary	Amy
3	Joyce	Sophie
4	Margaret	Charlotte
5	Dorothy	Laura
6	Doris	Lauren
7	Kathleen	Jessica
8	Irene	Hannah
9	Betty	Jade
10	Eileen	Emma

Accuracy in punctuation is vital, accuracy in spelling is highly desirable and a sure grasp of grammar is necessary. But we should not let the demands of accurate grammar affect our writing to the point where it becomes stilted and awkward.

As far as speech is concerned, we the users are the best judges – if we understand what is said to us and we can communicate efficiently in reply, then there is no more to be said about rightness and wrongness.

NOTES

COMMUNICATING ENGLISH

Handwriting

Word processing

The Internet

Handwriting

Good handwriting is an asset throughout your life. Its foundations are laid in the early years in school when the letter shapes and the ways they are joined in cursive writing are learnt.

Even so, it is never too late to make improvements. **You need to present written work that is neat, legible and attractive.** A sound investment is a good pen: one that is comfortable to hold and which writes evenly without too much pressure.

You have a choice of styles: looped lettering as in italic or copperplate; or unlooped. Whichever you prefer, you need to learn how letters are joined – all letters begin with an upstroke on the left and end with an upstroke on the right. This joining is what gives cursive writing its name and differentiates it from writing in capital letters. It is vital because it enables you to write at speed, an important attribute when you are keeping up with your thoughts!

THINK ABOUT IT

To achieve a good style you must learn the basic letter shapes for majuscules and minuscules, (capital and small letters). The way letters are joined needs to be learnt, for this is what gives cursive writing its name and differentiates it from printing. It is vital because it enables you to write at speed and keep up with your thoughts. You must practise.

NOTES

Word processing

Developments in computer technology have put word processing within the reach of most students and it is an invaluable aid to the English student. **A key feature of all GCSE courses is the folder of coursework and every board allows candidates to submit a proportion of their work in printed form.**

Furthermore, candidates are actively encouraged to draft and redraft their work but this can be a laborious process if you have to write everything in longhand. Every school has word-processing facilities and you should find out how you can use the equipment for your English coursework. You need keyboard skills as well, which is why it is very helpful if you have access to a computer at home to practise typing at speed.

NOTES

The Internet

The Internet is not a single network offering only one service, rather it is a network of networks offering a variety of different services, including e-mail, Usenet newsgroups and the World Wide Web (WWW or 'the net').

Net documents are transmitted using the 'hypertext transfer protocol' (http) and are most commonly generated by using 'hypertext mark-up language' (html) in a similar way to word processed documents. The material – text, sound, images – are mixed at the Internet location, the Uniform Resource Locators (URL).

N
O
T
E
S

Web pages are written by the same author or organisation on the same general subject and are organised into 'Web sites'. The starting page is known as the 'home page' from where you can 'navigate' the site by clicking the mouse on highlighted links. View the pages using computer applications called 'browsers', such as Microsoft Internet Explorer and Netscape. There is a great deal of jargon associated with the WWW but it is in fact quite easy to use.

NOTES

It is possible to tell a fair amount about a home page simply by knowing its URL. These addresses illustrate some of the conventions used in a URL:

http://***** is the opening for all addresses but the following suffixes indicate something about the author or organisation:

http://www.***********.com	an American based company (generally)
http://www.***********.au	a URL based in Australia
http://www.***********.nor	a URL based in Norway
http://www.***********.ir	a URL based in Ireland
http://www.***********.ac.uk	an academic institution based in the UK
http://www.***********.edu	an academic institution based in the USA
http://www.***********.gov	a government institution

Notice that US URLs generally do not have .us as their suffix since they have been the major contributors to the Web and are indeed the biggest consumers. A point to remember is that when the Americans are using the net, it takes longer to download documents.

N
O
T
E
S

If you want to use the net to find information, use a search engine or Web crawler. These are set up by Web-based companies such as AltaVista and they crawl through URLs, recording their contents on databases. You the Internet user can type in the word you are looking for and search its database for the information. When you do this you are working through the Web crawler's database by means of a 'cgi script' (a common gateway interface). Once the search has been completed, the search engine generates an html page with the results of your search.

Generally there will be a title list of sites on this page arranged in order of popularity, a brief summary of the content and a clickable link to the relevant site. If you find a particularly useful site, you can bookmark the address to revisit at a later date but remember the Web changes day by day and URLs can vanish as quickly as they have appeared.

For more information about the Web itself, future developments, standards and so on, try this URL – 'http://www.w3.org'

Handle Internet information with great care – it is often wrong!

The Internet is invaluable for research purposes but use it carefully. Don't just copy out chunks of material since its reliability cannot be guaranteed and material on the Internet is covered by copyright laws. You would be committing plagiarism. Moreover, good students are always selective in their use of source material.

NOTES

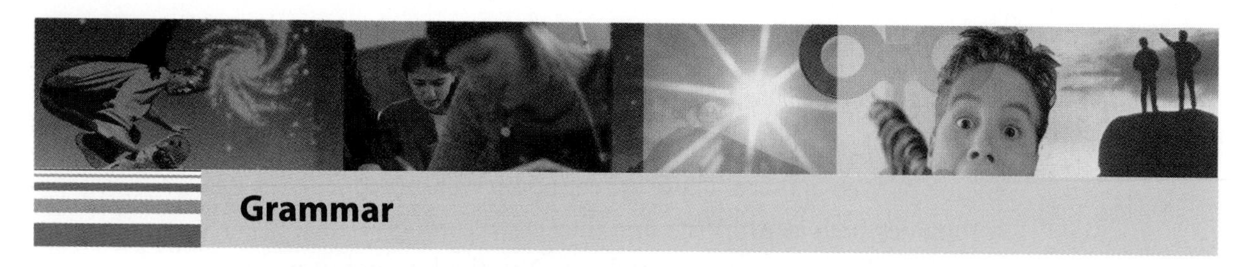

Grammar

Correct the following sentences:

1. Neither Peter nor Jane were there.
2. He was the man who's help we needed.
3. She is less noisier than I.
4. Next day, me and him went to town.
5. Have you been laying down for long?
6. Nobody loves you like I do, baby.
7. I know its right because I recognise it's shape.
8. These drinks are for you and I.
9. This Christmas, there are less shoppers in the West End.
10. This is the girl who I want to photograph.

Answers

1. Neither Peter nor Jane was there.
2. He was the man whose help we needed.
3. She is less noisy than me.
4. Next day, he and I went to town.
5. Have you been lying down for long?
6. Nobody loves you as I do, baby.
7. I know it's right because I recognise its shape.
8. These drinks are for you and me.
9. This Christmas there are fewer shoppers in the West End.
10. This is the girl whom I want to photograph.

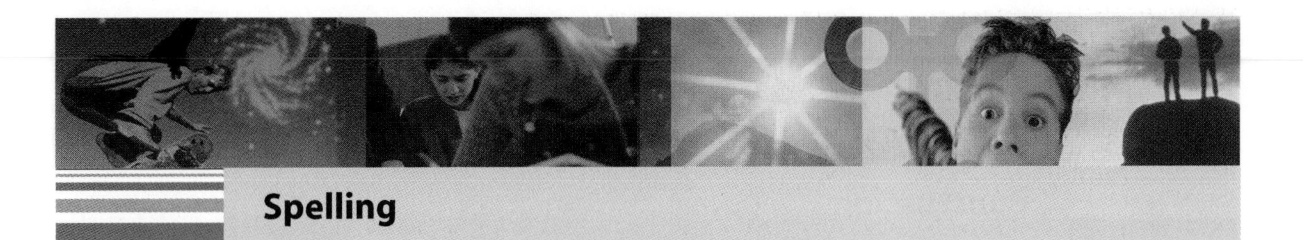

Spelling

Identify the words spelt incorrectly in these sentences:

1. He was a mischevious youngster who's wieird behavior in the stationary cupboard was as elicit as it was unneccessary!
2. My ninty-year-old nieghbour has a niece who hales from Middlesborough.
3. It is rediculous how long you have to cue at the doctor's for a proscription.
4. I am fully consious that my occaitional visits to the libray cause me personal inconvience.
5. The women was not aloud to spend much on stationary by her fiancée.

Identify which word best fits:

6. He was a — villain. (notable, notorious, noteworthy)
7. Always — what you preach. (practise, practice)
8. A — of schoolboys descended on the corner shop. (hoard, horde)
9. A critic should always aim to be —. (uninterested, disinterested)
10. By the time she had lost two stones, her — was minute. (waist, waste)

Answers

1. mischievous, whose, weird, behaviour, stationery, illicit, unnecessary
2. ninety, neighbour, hails, Middlesbrough
3. ridiculous, queue, prescription
4. conscious, occasional, library, inconvenience
5. woman, allowed, stationery, fiancé
6. notorious
7. practise
8. horde
9. disinterested
10. waist

Punctuation

Each of these sentences can be punctuated in two ways to change its meaning. Punctuate accordingly:

1. a woman without her man is useless
2. he said my friend was a waste of space
3. fancy cakes for tea
4. can you wait a minute while I wash katie
5. he attended to the last minute details
6. the manager said the shop assistant should be more polite
7. she thought richard was gorgeous
8. I like english history and geography lessons
9. meet bill james
10. the price was £5 less than I wanted

Answers

1. A woman without her man is useless.
   A woman – without her, man is useless.
2. He said my friend was a waste of space.
   'He,' said my friend, 'was a waste of space'.
3. Fancy cakes for tea.
   Fancy cakes for tea?
4. Can you wait a minute while I wash Katie?
   Can you wait a minute while I wash, Katie?
5. He attended to the last, minute details.
   He attended to the last-minute details.
6. The manager said the shop assistant should be more polite.
   'The manager,' said the shop assistant, 'should be more polite.'
7. She thought Richard was gorgeous.
   She, thought Richard, was gorgeous.
8. I like English history and geography lessons.
   I like English, history and geography lessons.
9. Meet Bill James.
   Meet Bill, James.
10. The price was £5 – less than I wanted.
    The price was £5 less than I wanted.

Language variation

The same words have different meaning in the US and the UK. Find the word which is defined in each of these sentences.

1. US: a room with a toilet
   UK: a room with a bathtub
2. US: a big failure
   UK: a great success
3. US: a non-alcoholic beverage made from apples
   UK: an alcoholic beverage made from apples
4. US: street level
   UK: one floor up from street level
5. US: 3.8 liters
   UK: 4.5 litres
6. US: short trousers
   UK: woman's undergarment
7. US: candle wax
   UK: oil distilled from petroleum
8. US: state school
   UK: private school
9. US: underground railway
   UK: underground walkway
10. US: wash hands and face
    UK: wash dishes after a meal

Answers

1. bathroom
2. bomb
3. cider
4. first floor
5. gallon
6. knickers
7. paraffin
8. public school
9. subway
10. wash up

General knowledge

What follows are the opening lines of different types of writing, novels, short stories, historical writing, plays, travel writing. See how much you can deduce from the information.

1. 'Little Man, would you come on? You keep it up and you're gonna make us late.'
2. There were no curtains up. The window was a hard edged block the colour of the night sky.
3. As we hear the musical introduction for the first song, we see Les, the Lollipop man, enter.
4. Everyone seemed to be going to China that year, or else writing rude things about the Arabs, or being frank about Africa.
5. First Lieutenant Jimmy Cross carried letters from a girl named Martha, a junior at Mount Sebastian College in New Jersey.
6. Mr Jones, of the Manor Farm, had locked the hen-houses for the night but was too drunk to remember to shut the pop-holes.
7. Well, as I was saying, The Emperor got into bed.
8. One day a morally righteous lawyer (admittedly an oxymoron) put Jesus' wisdom on trial.
9. We were coming down our road. Kevin stopped at a gate and bashed it with his stick.
10. He lay flat on the brown, pine-needled floor of the forest, his chin on his folded arms, and high overhead the wind blew in the tops of the pine trees.

Now pair each of the above with its closing line in these ten quotations:

A. His hand felt cold and big, dry and hard. 'Very well, thank you.'
B. He could feel his heart beating against the pine needle floor of the forest.
C. The Emperor immediately fell into a fit of catalepsy, in which he continued during the whole of that night and the greater part of the next day.

D. The lawyer immediately ran to the Jerusalem-to-Jericho road and began looking for victimised persons (potential clients) so he could enhance his income.

E. He buried the hawk in the field just behind the shed; went in, and went to bed.

F. The creatures outside looked from pig to man, and from man to pig, and from pig to man again; but already it was impossible to say which was which.

G. I'm skimming across the surface of my own history, moving fast, riding the melt beneath the blades, doing loops and spins, and when I take a high leap into the air and come down thirty years later, I realise it is as Tim trying to save Timmy's life with a story.

H. I started down the long pier towards the shore, trying to figure out a way of getting home.

I. No one can steal
Something you just feel
And although the picture fades
No one can take this time away

J. I cried for T.J. For T.J. and the land.

Answers

1. J *Roll of Thunder, Hear My Cry*, Mildred Taylor. (novel)
2. E *A Kestrel for a Knave*, Barry Hines. (novel)
3. I *Our Day Out*, Willy Russell. (play)
4. H *The Kingdom by the Sea*, Paul Theroux. (travel writing)
5. G *The Things They Carried*, Tim O'Brien. (Vietnam war book)
6. F *Animal Farm*, George Orwell. (allegorical novel)
7. C *Napoleon and the Spectre*, Charlotte Brontë. (short story)
8. D *Politically Correct Parables*, Robert Martin Walker. (short stories)
9. A *Paddy Clarke Ha Ha Ha*, Roddy Doyle. (an Irish childhood)
10. B *For Whom the Bell Tolls*, Ernest Hemingway. (novel set during the Spanish Civil War)

Index